# Norwegians

## IN WISCONSIN

Revised and Expanded Edition

Richard J. Fapso

THE WISCONSIN HISTORICAL SOCIETY PRESS

Madison

Published by the
Wisconsin Historical Society Press

© 2001 by The State Historical Society of Wisconsin

Photographs identified with PH, WHi, or VMA are from the Society's collections; send inquiries about such photos to the Curator, Visual Materials Archive, at the above address.

Publications of the Wisconsin Historical Society are available at quantity discounts for promotions, fund raising, and educational use. Write to the above address for more information.

Printed in the United States of America
Text and cover designed by Jane Tenenbaum Design
Photo research by Timothy Thering

05 04 03 02 01    5 4 3 2 1

**Library of Congress Cataloging-in-Publication Data**
Fapso, Richard J.
Norwegians in Wisconsin/Richard J. Fapso.—Rev. and expanded ed.
       p.  cm.
       ISBN 0-87020-334-7
1. Norwegian Americans—Wisconsin—History. 2. Wisconsin—History.
       3. Wisconsin—Ethnic relations. I. Title
       F590.S2 F36 2001
977.5'0043982—dc21                              2001020994
                                                    CIP

Et Skolehus. [Text i næste Nr.]

## ACKNOWLEDGMENTS

I especially wish to thank Theodore C. Blegen, Einar Haugen, and Carlton C. Qualey, who have contributed so much to the study of Norwegians in America. This book reflects their research and publications.

RICHARD J. FAPSO

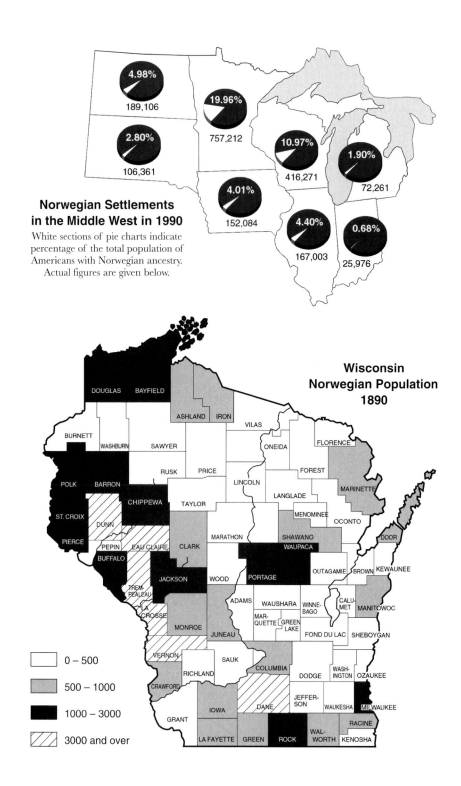

**Norwegian Settlements in the Middle West in 1990**

White sections of pie charts indicate percentage of the total population of Americans with Norwegian ancestry. Actual figures are given below.

4.98% — 189,106
2.80% — 106,361
19.96% — 757,212
4.01% — 152,084
10.97% — 416,271
1.90% — 72,261
4.40% — 167,003
0.68% — 25,976

**Wisconsin Norwegian Population 1890**

0 – 500
500 – 1000
1000 – 3000
3000 and over

## IN SEARCH OF NEW OPPORTUNITIES

Norway comprises the western and northern sections of the Scandinavian peninsula. Endowed with an extended coastline of well over 1,200 miles, it has since the days of the Vikings been traditionally recognized as a nation of seafarers. A rugged country with much of its south and central regions mountainous and its northern area so cold that it is considered tundra, Norway has little land area available for agriculture. In fact, three-fourths of the total land area cannot be cultivated, and the remaining one-quarter is mostly forested and grazing lands, with only 3 percent that could be cultivated in the early nineteenth century.

However, the nation's small percentage of arable land was, until late in the last century, home for more than 85 percent of its people, 53 percent of whom resided in the southeastern rolling meadowland, the only large area suited to agriculture. Another one-third or so lived along the tremendously extended and irregular coastline of the south and west, where *fjords* and other natural harbors had from earliest times been centers of fishing and trade.

In the mid-eighteenth century, with the introduction of the potato from the New World as a new source of food and with the lowering of the death rate through medical and sanitary advances, population began to increase all over Europe. Until 1815, Norway managed to absorb its share, but after that the rising birth rate exceeded the nation's capacity. Unlike England, which rapidly went from an agricultural to an industrial-mercantile society and acquired a new middle class, Norway changed very slowly. It remained agricultural, imprisoned by its geography. From 1815 forward, its population annually exceeded its agricultural productivity, and with no new opportunities available either on farms or in cities, many young people could not find work. But the expanding population was only one of a series of interrelated problems that eventually changed Norwegian society; others involved transportation, land ownership, the agricultural system, and the social class structure.

With the rise of industrialization, Europeans came increasingly to demand Norwegian natural resources. In response Norway enlarged its merchant marine, which not only expanded its role in international trade but also eventually provided the necessary transportation for emigrants for the New World.

During this period, Norwegians were also undergoing a change in their agricultural system. Like the rest of Europe, the country's agriculture was emerging from a self-contained semi-feudal system into a mercantile agriculture, based on the principle of cultivation for profit. In exchange for manufactured goods, Norway began exporting large amounts of agricultural products to the industrialized nations of Europe, and, as a direct result, traditional farming methods as generations had known them were radically transformed. For centuries farmers had become used to a system of land privately and rigidly controlled and to a shared common land. With the emerging pressures of population and the need to produce for a cash income, this system became obsolete, and landowners were no longer able to accommodate the cotters and landless day-laborers whose numbers more than doubled in the first half of the nineteenth century. With over three-fourths of the population engaged in agriculture in 1801, and still two-thirds in 1865, emigration became inevitable.

In addition, a number of fixed classes comprised this agricultural population: the *Bonder*, or freeholders, who can be divided into small and large landholders; the *Husmand*, or cotters; the day-laborers; and the servants. Unlike in earlier days, membership in the *bonder* class during the nineteenth century no longer gave one guarantee of economic security. The system of primogeniture, whereby the eldest son inherited the family farm, had been the accepted rule among this class. Primogeniture, combined with an increasing population, the lack of available new farm land, and fluctuating grain prices on the world market, brought many *Bonde* to financial ruin. Their sons and daughters, and even some of the landholders themselves, were forced to search for other opportunities. With every passing year increasing numbers looked more favorably toward America. It was this reason John L. Luraas from Telemark gave for leaving his native land: "I was my father's oldest son and consequently heir to the Luraas farm. It was regarded as one of the best in that neighborhood, but there was a $1,400 mortgage on it. I had worked for my father until I was twenty-five years old, and had no opportunity of getting money. It was plain to me, that I would have a hard time of it, if I should take the farm with the debt resting on it, pay a reasonable amount to my brothers and sisters and assume the care of my aged father. I saw to my horror how one farm after the other fell into the hands of the moneylenders, and this increased my dread of attempted farming. But I married and had to do something. Then it occurred to me that the best thing might be to emigrate to America. I was encouraged in this purpose by letters from Norwegian settlers in Illinois, written by a Norwegian emigrant who had lived two years in America. Such were the causes that led me to emigrate. . . ." The Luraas party left Norway on May 17, 1839, and arrived at Milwaukee seventeen weeks later.

*Husmand,* or cotters, considered themselves free men. It became virtually impossible, however, for these people to rise above their station of birth, and it was only the exceptional individual who achieved economic independence. *Husmand* owned little, renting their dwelling houses and a few acres of land from the *Bonde. Husmand,* as well as the day laborers and servants, suffered most from the economic and social disruption of the nineteenth century. To them the opportunity of obtaining land at low prices in America seemed almost too good to be true. During the nineteenth century thousands of Norwegians responded to the "American Fever," sold their meager possessions or were financed by benevolent *Bonder,* and sailed for the New World.

Modern Norwegian migration to America began in 1825, when the sloop *Restaurationen,* with fifty-three persons aboard, landed at New York. These early immigrants wrote letters to relatives and friends in the homeland, heightening interest in the New World. These "American letters" were eagerly read and often passed throughout villages and neighboring communities, spreading information about the United States and stirring interest in the prospects of emigration.

In 1835, one of the first immigrants to America returned to Norway. With the news of his arrival, people came from far and near to see and speak with this man. Through him many Norwegians received their first taste of "America Fever," and he unwittingly became one of the chief promoters of emigration. For many, this successful Norwegian American represented living proof of the opportunities to be had in the New World. In 1836, two ships carrying 160 people left Norway bound for new lives in America. The following year, two more ships departed, carrying 177 people, and the era of mass Norwegian migration had begun. Each succeeding year witnessed an increase in emigration, an increase so rapid that by 1860 nearly 70,000 Norwegians had emigrated to the United States.

Catering to the general interest, American guidebooks began appearing in Norway. Varying in quality and accuracy, these works advised the prospective immigrant on a wide range of topics. Although widely sold and extensively used by the majority who went to the New World, these books had little influence in motivating the reader actually to leave his home. The decision to emigrate, as well as determining where one would settle, proved to be most strongly influenced by friends or family members already in America, who reported back either in person or by letter.

Unlike some national groups to whom America offered a refuge from religious or political oppression, Norwegians suffered little persecution or discrimination in their homeland. Theirs was primarily a mass migration of agricultural people compelled by adverse conditions of land and climate and the emerging pressures of the Industrial Revolution to leave Norway in search of new homes and futures on other, more hospitable shores.

In earlier years neither Bergen nor any other Norwegian port provided transportation to America. Emigrants either purchased a vessel themselves, as some organized groups did, or journeyed to Goteborg in Sweden, Hamburg in Germany, Le Havre in France, or some other European port from which they could set sail.

At the beginning of the nineteenth century, Norwegian merchants became aware of the possibilities in trade with North American ports. America's rapidly expanding industries produced such a growing need for iron that by the mid-1840s, the United States emerged as the chief importer of Norwegian ore. Norway in return imported American cotton, flour, rice, tobacco, rye, logwood, resin, and other natural resources. The opening of this Norwegian-American trade not only provided a means for emigrants to travel directly to America, but also channeled Norwegians to the northern industrial ports of the United States: New York, New Haven, Boston, and Baltimore. Similarly, with the opening of the Norwegian trade with Canada in the 1850s, Quebec became a major port of debarkation.

# THE DIFFICULT JOURNEY

Twenty-nine Norwegian merchant vessels arrived in New York in 1847. Ten came directly from Norway, carrying both immigrants and iron in an often stormy Atlantic crossing that took anywhere from six to twelve weeks. For most the voyage was not a pleasant one, since conditions aboard ship were primitive and uncomfortable. Normally two rows of bunks of rough boards were constructed, one above the other, the whole length of the ship. Light came through open hatchways and partly through skylights in the deck, but when storms came, no light at all was admitted, and the passengers were quite frequently shut up in the poorly lit rooms for days waiting for a storm to subside.

Supplies for the journey consisted of smoked and salted meat, flat bread, dried peas and beans, and many large casks of fresh water. In fair weather cookhouses were set up on deck. When the weather turned stormy, however, it became difficult for anybody to use cooking facilities, and the voyagers had to content themselves with cold uncooked meals.

On the open Atlantic, seasickness affected nearly all immigrants. This, however, was a minor discomfort compared to the outbreaks of disease that sometimes occurred in midocean. Many ship captains made great efforts to combat disease during the voyage, but given the crowded conditions, it was impossible to contain the spread of a highly contagious disease. Cholera, smallpox, typhoid fever, and measles were some of the maladies that broke out on immigrant vessels. Of the ships arriving at Quebec in 1861, one reported forty-seven passengers dead and sixty seriously ill; another ship had thirty-three dead, mostly children under six who had succumbed to measles.

In spite of the discomforts and dangers experienced throughout the length of the voyage, there were also times of joy and relaxation. "When the weather was fine and the Atlantic lay clear and smooth, the deck at times rang with meriment in the evenings," wrote Norwegian-American historian Theodore C. Blegen in his *Land of Their Choice.* Sunday was always a special day. In fair weather prayers and devotion would be held above deck and the singing of hymns might be accompanied by a flute, violin, or other musical instrument.

Arrival in America after the long voyage was an exciting moment. For most, however, their welcome was not what they expected, as con men and swindlers of every kind descended upon them. As a result, some unwarned immigrants found themselves penniless and were forced to find employment in their port of entry. In later years, Wisconsin's establishment of a state board of commissioners of immigration in New York and a central depot for immigration at Castle Gardens represented attempts to protect the arriving foreigners. The majority of Norwegians, however, had their destinations fixed before their arrival in the New World. Most set out immediately to join friends or relatives in the Midwest.

After leaving New York for a journey to Wisconsin, for example, the immigrants went by steamboat up the Hudson River to Albany, where they transferred to canal boats bound for Buffalo and finally booked passage on a Great Lakes sailing vessel for Chicago or Milwaukee. In the mid-1850s the stream of Norwegian migration shifted from New York to Quebec, but even though they arrived in Canada, most soon headed for Norwegian settlement areas in the American Midwest. From Quebec they traveled by riverboat to Buffalo, at which point they linked up with their countrymen arriving from New York, continuing on by means of ship or rail to states like Wisconsin.

Travel time from eastern ports to Milwaukee or Chicago ranged between seven and ten days. These final days of the journey proved to be the most difficult and dangerous segment of the entire trip. Swindlers and frauds continued to greet them at every stop and the crowding on canal and lake boats was so intense that the immigrants were shoved in like baggage. With the completion of the railroad to Chicago in the 1850s, travel time and discomfort were reduced.

## WISCONSIN SETTLEMENT

The earliest Norwegian settlers in the Midwest established farm communities in the Fox River valley region in Illinois. Some of these first settlements turned out to be unsuccessful, since the land selected was low-lying and poorly drained. In 1837 an epidemic of malarial fever swept through a number of settlements as the spring rains and thaws turned crop lands into disease-breeding swamps. By the late 1830s, however, the American frontier had gone beyond Illinois, moving northward and westward into Wisconsin. Survivors from the less successful Norwegian settlements in Illinois, along with newly arrived immigrants, now began to seek land in Wisconsin Territory.

The first Norwegian settler on Wisconsin soil was Ole Nattestad, who had arrived in America in 1837 and had initially settled in Illinois. Dissatisfied with its marshy land and unhealthy climate, he set out in search of better farming and country to the northwest. The journey led him across the Wisconsin-Illinois line, and on July 1, 1838, he staked an eighty-acre claim on the Jefferson Prairie in Rock County. In the following year his brother Ansten arrived, bringing with him a group of emigrants from the brothers' home district of Numedal. Several families of this group settled to the west of Jefferson Prairie in an area known as Rock Prairie, where the land was well drained and fertile. As a result, the sector became a cluster of Norwegian settlements, eventually expanding over both sides of the state line. By 1850 the entire Rock Prairie settlement boasted a population of 180 families totaling 942 persons. These initial colonies led the way for continued Norwegian immigration to Wisconsin. Functioning as important depots, they became the immediate destination of a large percentage of Norwegian immigrants steadily moving northwestward into the expanding frontier.

During the same time that Rock Prairie was being settled, Norwegians established another significant settlement in southeastern Waukesha County and northwestern Racine County. In the summer of 1839, forty people from Upper Telemarken, together with twenty from Stavanger, took passage on a cargo ship bound for Boston. Reaching America safely, they proceeded westward by way of the Erie Canal and the Great Lakes to Milwaukee. On arrival the group heard of a terrible malaria epidemic in the Illinois settlements and decided to locate instead in an area in Waukesha County near Lake Muskego, from which the settlement took its name.

In the summer, when the land was dry, Muskego looked well drained and fertile. With the arrival of the spring rains, however, the land became swampy. During the first year no malaria appeared in this settlement, but the following two years, especially after a rapid increase in population in 1843, a general epidemic swept the colony. This debilitating fever, or "ague" as it was sometimes called, was followed by worse plagues in the years 1849, 1850, and 1852, when a series of deadly cholera outbreaks took the lives of hundreds in the Muskego region.

Muskego became important because it lies close to Milwaukee, a major port of entry in the 1840s and 1850s for Norwegian immigrants bound for the northwestern frontier. For them, the Muskego settlement was looked upon as a haven for the travel-weary, and every summer the colony was filled with newly arrived immigrants hoping to stop for a while, rest, and seek advice.

Among its early residents, Muskego had a surprising number of famous Norwegian Americans. Elling Eielsen, the first Lutheran pastor in America, eventually became the organizer of the first Lutheran Norwegian-American Lutheran Synod. Claus Clausen, although a Dane, came to Muskego to teach in the parochial school. During his life he helped organize four synods and became the editor of two important Norwegian-American newspapers. Even Heg was well known as a lay preacher and provider for many Norwegians who came through Muskego on their way westward. His son, Hans C. Heg, became a colonel in the Fifteenth Wisconsin Volunteer Infantry, a Civil War regiment whose membership was over 90 percent Norwegian. James Denoon Reymert, a founding editor of the first Norwegian newspaper in America, *Nordlyset*, lived in Muskego from 1847 to 1849. Reymert was also a member of Wisconsin's constitutional convention and the first Norwegian American to hold a state office. But because of the unhealthiness of the area, Muskego never assumed the significance its location and eminent leaders would seem to have warranted.

Directly to the west of Muskego, Norwegian pioneers in 1840 established the third and most successful of the early colonies. Named Koshkonong, it was located in the fertile agricultural region of southeastern Dane and western Jefferson Counties. This area quickly earned the distinction of being better than any of the earlier settlements. Reports of its fertile soil, extensive grazing land, and abundance of wood for fuel and lumber spread throughout the Midwest. Into this region flowed not only hundreds of newly arrived Norwegians, but also many from the older communities of Rock Prairie, Muskego, and Illinois. The colony grew so rapidly that by 1850 it covered over twelve townships in the two-county region, with a population of 543 Norwegian families totaling 2,670 persons.

With the settlement of the Koshkonong region, the first half of Norwegian settlement in Wisconsin was complete. Within a twelve-year span, four significant Norwegian colonies had been established: Jefferson Prairie, Rock Prairie, Muskego, and Koshkonong. Between the years 1838 and 1855, these settlements served as centers of information, aid, and general destination points for the Norwegian migratory movement in America. In the years following, these older settlements continued to provide a necessary service: Acting as mother colonies, they fostered the growth of new settlements in western Wisconsin, Iowa, and Minnesota. This manner of settlement became an established pattern common to the Norwegian experience in America. With the ever-expanding frontier, each new settlement became a point of dispersion from which newly arriving immigrants leapfrogged their way ever north and westward.

A number of smaller colonies outside of the mainstream of Norwegian settlement can be found in northeastern and north-central Wisconsin. A fairly large group of Norwegians settled in Manitowoc County around the year 1848. Although Germans had already settled heavily in this region, Norwegians found the location, with its fertile land and its port city of Manitowoc, an ideal area in which to locate. Concentrating mostly in Manitowoc and the townships of Cato, Eaton, Liberty, Rapids, and Rockland, the Norwegian population grew from 203 in 1850 to 2,468 in 1870.

Settlements in north-central Wisconsin appeared as early as 1848 when a number of Norwegians moved into Winnebago County. The largest area of Norwegian settlement in north-central Wisconsin, however, is located in Portage and Waupaca Counties. Arriving in 1850, these first immigrants named the region *Indi-landet*. Unlike southern Wisconsin, large tracts in this region could still be purchased at the low government price of $1.25 an acre. Many took advantage of this opportunity, and by the late 1860s nearly six townships in these two counties were composed entirely of Norwegians. The settlements covered the townships of Amherst and New Hope, the city of Stevens Point in Portage County, and the towns of Scandinavia, Saint Lawrence, and Iola in Waupaca County.

Other areas of settlement include a small colony in Marathon County, a scattering in Green Lake and Marquette Counties, and a more well-defined region in Adams and Juneau Counties. The settlements in northeastern and north-central Wisconsin, however, appear small and diffuse in comparison to the large and well-defined region in southeastern and southern Wisconsin. Although immigration into these

areas increased in the late nineteenth century, it never attained great significance, and these localities remained outside of the mainstream of
Norwegian settlement.

During the time Norwegians were settling southern Wisconsin,
improvements occurred in transportation that helped open the frontier
to the north and west. The first rail line in the state, completed in 1851,
ran only twenty miles. From that year on, however, railroad construction
extended ever westward until in 1857 a rail line stretched from Milwaukee to the Mississippi River. The importance of the railroad to nineteenth-century rural Wisconsin cannot be overestimated, as it gave
farmers in remote areas the opportunity to sell their crops in the eastern
markets. The railroad also had a significant effect on the second phase of
Norwegian settlement.

By 1850, the most fertile land in southern and eastern Wisconsin
had been taken. Norwegians, seeking desirable farm lands at low prices,
had no alternative but to move farther west. With the establishment of
the Blue Mounds settlement in western Dane County in 1848, Norwegian pioneers began moving into what would soon become another
extensive Norwegian settlement. By 1870 the area of their settlement
would cover a seventeen-county zone stretching from Crawford and
Dane Counties and would, by 1900, make Norwegians the second
largest ethnic group in Wisconsin.

During the same year that they established the settlement at Blue
Mounds, Norwegians began staking claims in the fertile soil of Crawford and Vernon Counties. Except for small villages along the Mississippi River, settlers in the year 1848 found these western regions uninhabit-
ed. Adequate overland transportation into the area was also nonexistent.
Instead settlers relied on boats plying the Wisconsin and Mississippi
Rivers. These first arrivals came from the Muskego and Koshkonong
regions and were soon followed by immigrants coming directly from
Norway. The census of 1850 indicated only a handful of Norwegians in
the vicinity of Prairie du Chien, but by 1860 well over four hundred
were present, settling mainly in the northern townships of Crawford
County.

Vernon County, which contains the famous Coon Valley and Coon
Prairie settlements, claims to be the most densely settled Norwegian area
in the state. Norwegians from the Muskego and Koshkonong regions
were again the first settlers. Arriving as early as 1848, they blazed the

way for the thousands who would come later. Coon Valley's steep hills and fertile valleys struck early immigrants with its beauty and its vague similarity to Norway, prompting enthusiastic letters home, urging others to follow. Hundreds arrived, filling the region and creating the most distinctly Norwegian settlement in western Wisconsin.

Moving north, settlers from Dane County reached La Crosse in 1850. The city, a river port and soon to be rail depot, attracted hundreds of Norwegians. By 1858 the railroad linked La Crosse with Milwaukee, and the northern city became a major depot for immigrants. While many Norwegians remained in the city, others acquired land, chiefly in the townships of Bangor, Barre, Farmington, Greenfield, Holland, Neshonoc, Onalaska, and Washington. The Norwegian population in La Crosse County increased from 1,347 in 1860 to 3,381 in 1870, overflowing into the adjoining counties of Monroe and Jackson to the east and north.

Settlement in Trempealeau Valley in Trempealeau and Jackson Counties constitutes a unit of settlement apart from the southern colonies. The settlers came here directly from Norway in 1852. After stopping at Coon Valley for a short period, they moved directly into the Trempealeau Valley. With the establishment of the initial settlement, the valley gradually filled with Norwegians and continues to be predominantly Norwegian American today.

With the start of the Civil War, immigration receded and did not pick up again until 1865. By then the mainstream of Norwegian immigration had shifted farther west. The Homestead Act of 1862 opened vast stretches of land in Iowa and Minnesota to settlement, and Wisconsin no longer held a monopoly on Norwegian immigrants. Norwegians, however, continued to flow into the state, and many began pioneering in the northwestern regions. The attraction to this area lay in the immediate opportunity for work, with the lumber industry employing the majority of these later arrivals.

Agricultural activity in Barron, Polk, St. Croix, and Dunn Counties did not begin in earnest until the 1870s, when scattered groups of Norwegians began moving into Douglas and Bayfield Counties. The principal areas of the second phase of Norwegian migration to the state had been fixed by 1850s, and by 1890 well over 30,000 Norwegians inhabited a chain of counties running from Crawford County in the south to Dunn in the north.

Norwegian Lutheran Church, Crawford County.

The first Norwegian church in Wisconsin, built at Muskego in 1844. Claus Lauritz Clausen had organized this congregation the previous winter and served as its first minister. Until the church was built, the initial two hundred Norwegian souls who joined the congregation met in Even Heg's barn.

The Christian and Marit Anderson farm, Springdale Township (Dane County), 1894. Although the barn and log trough were out of date by the time of this photo, the Andersons had joined Wisconsin's agricultural mainstream—the dual-purpose milk-and-meat cattle on the left were being phased out by the milk-producing Holsteins at right.

The Valdres, Norway, home of Christian Anderson, c. 1900. In 1857, Anderson, age 16, immigrated to America with his family, settling first in Black Earth and later in Springdale Township (Dane County).

Name File, VMA                                Name File, VMA

Ole Nattestad (left) arrived in America in 1837, initially settling in Illinois. Dissatis-fied with the land and climate, he staked a claim in Rock County on July 1, 1838, becoming Wisconsin's first Norwegian settler. The following year his brother, Ansten (right), followed him to Wisconsin. Ansten brought along a large group of fellow Norwegians, most from Numedal and northern Telemark.

Andreas Dahl Collection: Ph 4256 (neg. WHi D3 71), VMA

Scene from a Norwegian-American wedding outside the old Norway Grove Church, rural DeForest, 1875. The photograph was taken by Norwegian-American Andreas Dahl (1844–1923). Dahl came to Wisconsin from Valdres, Norway, in 1869 and became an itinerate photographer. His photographs, most taken in the mid-1870s, concentrated on capturing the work, home, and community lives of Norwegians in Wisconsin.

Name file, VMA

Colonel Hans Christian Heg of the Fifteenth Wisconsin Volunteer Infantry. Heg was born in Lier, Norway, and immigrated to Muskego in 1840. He died in September 1863 from wounds sustained at the battle of Chickamauga. The Fifteenth's membership was over 90 percent Norwegian; Heg was instrumental in recruiting volunteers.

The Hans Christian Heg statue greets visitors to the Wisconsin State Capitol at the King Street entrance. The statue was sculpted by Paul Fjelde and presented to the State of Wisconsin by the Norwegian Society of America in 1925. This photo was taken in the mid-1940s.

Lot 2361 Box 1, VMA        Lot 2361 Box 1, VMA

Norwegian-American Civil War veterans. *Left:* Carl Tjorbjornsen was born May 25, 1843, in Telemark and immigrated to Wisconsin in 1847. A corporal in Company C of the Fifteenth Wisconsin Volunteer Infantry, he was entered on the Roll of Honor for bravery in December 1862. The C and 15 on his stole denote his company and regiment. Members of Company C called themselves the "Norway Bear Hunters." *Right:* Sergeant Albert Emmonson, born in Norway Township (Racine County), also of Company C, was cited for bravery in battle at Chickamauga in 1863.

Lot 2361 Box 1, VMA        Lot 2361 Box 2, VMA

*Left:* Corporal Erick N. Basness (Baroness), a member of Company B of the Fifteenth WVI, was born in Sogndal, Norway, in 1841 and immigrated to America in 1861; he enlisted later that same year. The men of Company B referred to themselves as the "Wergeland Guards" after the famous Norwegian writer and poet Henrick Wergeland. *Right:* John H. Johnson of Primrose became the Fifteenth's chaplain in October of 1864.

# Billed-Magazin.

No. 35.]     Madison, Wisconsin den 31te Juli.     [1869.

## "Old Abe".

Under Krigen mod Rebellerne, opmuntredes blandt Soldaterne under Vaabenstilstanden, allehaande Forsøg til Tidsfordriv; Musikchor, Sangforeninger, Turnforeninger og kortsagt allehaande Lege, der kunde bibringe Soldaten en livlig Sindsstemning, til Afverling fra de dødbringende Slag, og de lange og besværlige Marscher.

Allerede ved Oprettelse af nye Regimenter, gjordes Forberedelser beregnet paa Tidsfordriv blandt Soldaterne. Vi finde saaledes hos det 8de Wisconsin Regiment en levende Ørn, som af Kaptein Parkins Kompagni C blev givet Navnet "Old Abe" efter den daværende Præsident Abraham Lincoln.

Der fortælles om denne Ørn, (af hvem vi idag leverer et Billede), at den blev fanget 1861 i Chipaway County i Wisconsin, af en Indianer, ved Navn Age-moh-me-ge-zhig, som solgte den til en Mr. D. McCann for en Bushel Mais. Ørnen var dengang to Aar gammel, og blev kjøbt af det nylig organiserede Kompagni C af 8de Wisconsin Regiment for den billige Pris 2½ Dollars. Ørnen fulgte Kompagniet til Madison, hvor den i Camp Randal blev modtaget med stor Begeistring af 8de Regiment.

"Old Abe".

Ved Regimentets Gjennemmarsch i Chicago og St. Louis, tiltrak den levende Ørn, der blev baaret paa et med nationale Kulører smykket Stativ, sig Alles Opmærksomhed.

Ved enhver Anledning under Soldaternes Raab syntes "Old Abe" at tage livlig Del i Begeistringen og selv under den stærkeste Kugleregn syntes "Abe" at inspirere de tappre Gutter af Wisconsins 8de Regiment.

Ørnen har bivaanet 22 Slag foruden mange smaa Træfninger og mærkelig nok ikke en, af de Mange som sigtedes om at bære "Old Abe" har været rammet af Fiendens Kugler.

Den 16de September 1864 udmønstredes "Old Abe" af Onkle Sams Krigshær, og blev af Regimentet foræret til Staten Wisconsin, som nu giver den Pension, bestaaende af Høns og Duer som den med største Behagelighed fortærer, i den nederste Etage af Statens smukke Kapitolinm i Madison.

Ørnen er nu en Kuriositet for Fremmede, der besøger Madison, og om Sommeren vil man ofte se "Old Abe" i Kapitol-Parken meget rolig hensat i Erindringen om svundne Tider.

A front page from *Billed-Magazin*, the first illustrated Norwegian-American magazine, published in Madison from 1868 to 1870. Svein Nilsson edited the journal. His articles often documented the lives of Norwegian immigrants in Wisconsin.

Andreas Dahl Collection: PH 4251 (WHi D31 208), VMA

The Halvor Nerison Hauge farm, Christiana Township (Dane County), c. 1875. Hauge was a prominent dairy farmer.

Andreas Dahl Collection: PH 4251 (WHi D31 174), VMA

Wheat farmers at Koshkonong, c. 1875.

## ADAPTATION AND CHANGE

Being an immigrant to a new land, knowing neither the language nor the customs and faced with the daily struggle for the survival on the Wisconsin frontier, was undoubtedly a frightening experience for the average person. Many became convinced that settling among other Norwegians was not only wise but necessary. Within this difficult and foreign environment it gave immigrants comfort to have people around them who had a common heritage, spoke the same language, and shared and understood their thoughts. The settlements of Koshkonong, Muskego, Coon Valley, and others resulted from this natural human need to seek comfort and security from friends and neighbors in unfamiliar surroundings. After the long journey across the Atlantic into the interior of America, finally reaching a Norwegian colony warmed the heart and lifted the spirits. Many of the smaller settlements often grew up around a nucleus of people from the same district or even the same family. In such settlements as farming communities on the frontier, having Norwegian neighbors postponed and cushioned the shock of adjusting to a strange and often baffling land. The necessity of reshaping one's whole life and personality was a transition that could best be made a step at a time.

In the larger settlements some people actually continued to live virtually as they had in Norway. English remained a foreign language. Yet English was the language of the land, and sooner or later everyone had to learn it. Ignorance of the language was a great handicap to the Norwegian immigrant, wrote Ole Rynning in his guide book, "especially on the trip to the interior of the country."

Rynning continued: "Before having learned the language fairly well, one must not expect to receive so large a daily or yearly wage as the native-born American." Norwegian immigrants soon realized that learning English was the key to economic survival. Besides helping them secure employment, it was also essential for such business dealings as the purchase of land and the marketing of crops.

Unlike immigrants from eastern or southern Europe, the Scandinavians had the advantage of a certain similarity in vocabulary and word structure between American speech and their own. This fact made the linguistic transition relatively easy for Norwegians. At first they could simply mix English words into their sentences, but as time went on, they transformed their speech into acceptable English.

Immigrant farmers had to learn an entirely new vocabulary, since American agricultural conditions and landscape exhibited few similarities to those of the homeland. Having little money, a majority of Norwegian immigrants hired themselves out in the first years as farm laborers; working for a prosperous Yankee farmer taught them more than just the English language. They learned about new American crops and agricultural methods. Tobacco, for instance, initially a Yankee cash crop, quickly became associated with Norwegians as they adopted the growing methods of their American neighbors. The fertile land in the Koshkonong settlement proved to be ideal for tobacco, and consequently an association between tobacco cultivation and Norwegians in Wisconsin remains evident to this day.

Immigrants had to add to their vocabulary the American terms for local farming practices, as well as the words for unfamiliar crops. Norwegian farmers had no names of their own for the modern American farm machinery and so had to learn them. Even those who never actually became fluent in English learned the words for the most important new objects and ideas that confronted them on every hand, quite often giving them a Norwegian pronunciation and Norwegian grammatical forms.

Language was not the only cultural barrier the immigrants faced; they soon discovered they had to adjust to new modes of dress as well. Letters from America spoke of the difference between the clothes worn in the New World and those of Norway. Some went on to advise prospective emigrants to bring little Old World clothing. The need to conform to American standards of dress can be clearly understood, for as one immigrant wrote: "A new comer can immediately be detected by his garb, and since newcomers are regarded with very little esteem, all of them proceed at once to buy clothes of an American cut."

Those who heeded such advice found themselves unprepared for the extremes of the Midwestern climate. Later arrivals, mindful of the miscalculations of others before them, chose the contents of their immigrant trunks with greater care. Beginning in the 1850s, improvements in transportation allowed these later immigrants to carry more "necessities." Immigrants no longer left sheepskin coats, woolen pants, and a pair of sturdy boots at home. Quite often, they brought an extra coat, a pair of pants, or a spool of woolen yarn at the request of a relative or friend in America. They might also bring from Norway small mechanical items that were considered too expensive or of poorer quality in America.

Norwegian immigrants were unaccustomed to American-made clothes. Preferring their traditional system of having things made to order at home, they considered manufactured clothes inferior. Such complaints were not totally unfounded, since much of the American-made clothing available on the frontier offered little selection and low quality and generally was expensive. With the improvement in transportation and the introduction of mail-order catalogs, clothing quality improved and prices became more competitive; as time went on most immigrants grew accustomed to American clothes. Farmers and artisans wore jeans and work shirts in the summer. In the winter, red flannel underwear, corduroy pants, and sheepskin coats became the accepted style.

Women's clothing on the frontier tended to be drab and utilitarian. Except for a few small items, Norwegians abandoned their native costumes, since certain fabrics and bright-colored materials were not available. Norwegian women preferred wool and linen fabrics in making clothes. American wool was considered inferior by Norwegian standards and linen was seldom available, as Americans tended to rely heavily on cotton goods. Yankee puritan influence also proved to be a factor, since gay costumes were associated with the sins of pride and vanity. The mood of the day expressed the belief: the plainer the costume, the more pleasing it was to the Almighty.

During the early period of the Norwegian-American experience, little opportunity existed for expressing the refinements of one's cultural heritage. Yet many brought with them beautiful specimens of Norwegian arts and handicrafts such as the breastpins and brooches designed to be worn with folk costumes among all classes of Norwegian society. Those with more means, like the *Bonder,* brought their wedding costumes, handsomely embroidered garments worn by both men and women and containing deep religious and cultural significance. Handed down from one generation to another, these costumes became family treasures that, if space allowed, were taken to the New World.

These examples of Old World art and handicraft were never used to the extent that was customary in Norway. Although Norwegian immigrants continued to celebrate their traditional holidays and feast days, the wearing of obvious festive dress and costume was, for the most part, abandoned. It was not until the twentieth century, with the rise of ethnic consciousness among later generations, that these costumes again became popular for folk dances and gala entertainments, such as the annual Syttende Mai celebration in Stoughton.

Adjusting to American food was oftentimes an unpleasant experience for the newly arrived immigrant. Norwegians found the American diet quite different from their accustomed milk and porridge, flat bread, *lefse* (unleavened potato bread), dried meat, and fish; many found it difficult to adjust. The American emphasis on pork was widely considered to be responsible for much sickness among the immigrants. A Norwegian who journeyed to Wisconsin observed: "The large amount of pork which the Americans use is not good for people unaccustomed to such a heavy diet. . . . Our (Norwegian) farmers from the uplands think it is a fine food, but in a warm climate, used in excess, it is very injurious, especially when eaten without an abundance of vegetables.

However, others found the new American diet a considerable improvement over their native foods. "I want you to know, dear brother," wrote one immigrant, "that I am enthusiastic about America and that we are all flourishing here. . . . Every meal, I sit down to a table loaded with good things, as good, I may say, as any of the delicacies set before guests in Norway."

The immigrant's daily reliance on pork as a major source of food was, if not unhealthy, surely a monotonous practice. Consuming pork once, twice, or three times a day soon blunted its appeal. As one's lot in America improved, new meats replaced pork. Beef, veal, mutton, and lamb became part of the immigrant's fare. In addition to learning to prepare these new additions "American style," the immigrants began to reinstitute their own culinary customs.

Dairy products are also important in the Norwegian diet. The heat of the Wisconsin summer, however, made the preservation of dairy products almost impossible. Being unaware of the Midwestern climate before their arrival, immigrants learned of this limitation through bitter experience. "I remember I used to wonder, " remarked a Norwegian woman, "when I heard that it would be impossible to use milk here as we did at home, but I certainly have discovered that it is true. It is so hot here in summer that it is impossible to work it into cheese. . . . It is futile to try to make cheese in the early summer; during the fall, however, it is possible to keep it."

In the early period the immigrants sorely missed many traditional foods that were unavailable in pioneer Wisconsin. To compensate for this deficiency, products common in America but unknown or too expensive in Norway now became accessible. Coffee, for example, found ready acceptance and in fact became so popular that coffee drinking quickly assumed the rank of an established social institution among Norwegian Americans. Norwegians were also delighted with the variety of American sweets. Sugar, in limited supply in Norway, could be found in abundance. Sweetening could be derived from a number of different sources in the form of molasses, maple syrup, and honey, all easily available in Wisconsin, or from sugar cane grown in the southern United States. Candy, sweet cakes, and pies soon became common items in the Norwegian diet.

But as radically as frontier conditions initially altered immigrants' eating habits, old food preferences reasserted themselves when the occasion allowed. With the planting of crops of rye, barley, and oats, flat bread again appeared on the family table; when potato flour became available, Norwegian housewives returned to baking *lefse*. Old Country dishes continued to be served wherever Norwegian Americans sat down to eat, in later years becoming holiday foods linking the present with the past and symbolizing the spirit of Norwegian nationality.

## RELIGION AND SCHOOLS

Many church officials in Norway disagreed with the ever-increasing number of parishioners who wished to emigrate to America, emphasizing the physical and spiritual dangers facing those who left the homeland. Because of this stand, there were no churches in most of the frontier areas where the first Norwegians settled.

As a temporary measure, the practice of lay preaching was carried on among the immigrants during the early period of the Wisconsin frontier. One such lay preacher was Even Heg, who arrived at the Muskego settlement in 1840. Heg not only preached but also baptized hundreds of babies in Muskego and the surrounding territory. Years later, when an officially ordained minister did arrive, Heg discontinued baptizing, though he continued to preach and perform community services. Before the minister's arrival Heg had built a large barn in which religious services could be held. This structure also served as a resting place for many Norwegian newcomers passing through Muskego on their way westward in search of land, and during the summer months the barn was often crowded to capacity with guests. Some of them stayed only a few days; others prolonged their visit for a month or more. The building also served as a hospital when the fearful cholera epidemics of 1849, 1850, and 1852 swept the area.

It was at this Muskego settlement that the beginnings of a formal Norwegian American Lutheran church took place. Norwegian settlers built and occupied the first regular church building here in 1844. Children in the area could now receive religious training similar to that given by the schools of Norway, while adults could receive the advice and services that only an ordained minister could give them.

To care for the spiritual needs of the ever-increasing number of immigrants, the Norwegian-American church realized it must expand. With the pressing need, and in view of the continued lack of interest on the part of the church officials in Norway, Americanized pastors saw that clergy would have to come from the American settlements. The Norwegian Synod decided in 1861 to establish a college for the training of ministers. The new school, begun in Wisconsin in 1862, was later moved to Decorah, Iowa, where it became Luther College.

The Norwegian Synod, with its new body of university-trained leaders, soon became a well-organized and disciplined religious institution. Members of its clergy, however, representing the most conservative elements within the Norwegian Lutheran Church, often expressed views that were widely unpopular among the Norwegian immigrants. One example that illustrates this situation can be seen in the public school controversy that raged from the early pioneer era through the 1880s.

The Wisconsin Constitution of 1848 provided for a system of public schools "free and without charge for tuition," and as the system developed, education came within the reach of all. English was the common language in which children from the various ethnic groups within each school district were taught the 3 R's. Desiring that their children learn English and become familiar with American institutions, the majority of Norwegians actively supported the public school system. The Synod, however, interpreted state-supported instruction as a threat. Feeling that public schools were religionless and were centers of dangerous influences from which Lutheran youth should be guarded, the Synod demanded that parochial schools replace the common schools, a stand that resulted in a long and bitter controversy among all members of the various Norwegian Lutheran churches.

Led by the Norwegian-American press and a group of outspoken laymen, the average Norwegian immigrant rejected the Synod's plea for parochial schools and quietly accepted the public system. Since the founding of the first Norwegian Lutheran church in America, internal controversies such as this often resulted in splits within the church. The extreme Lutheran orthodoxy of the Norwegian Synod led many to seek other Lutheran bodies that appeared less inflexible and more sensitive to the new ways of American life.

While Lutherans dominated the life of the Norwegian community they never absorbed all the immigrants, many of whom became attracted to other religious orders. For example, the oldest Scandinavian Methodist Church in the world was established among the Norwegians of Cambridge, Wisconsin, in 1851. At Pine Lake, Wisconsin, the famous Swedish pastor Gustaf Unonius persuaded many Norwegians to join his Episcopal church in the 1840s. In 1853, an attempt was made to establish a Moravian communistic community in Ephraim, Wisconsin. Nils Otto Tank, the original leader of the community, succeeded in attracting many of his fellow Norwegians to Ephraim.

## THE IMMIGRANT PRESS

Another institution of major influence on Norwegian group life in America was the Norwegian-American press. Newly arrived immigrants, however, were not accustomed to American journalistic traditions. In nineteenth-century Norway, newspapers were few, expensive, and of little interest to the general public. Although literacy was relatively high, the common farmer did not concern himself with questions of public affairs outside his own parish or village. Overcoming this feeling of indifference among the immigrants was the biggest obstacle for the founders of the Norwegian-American press.

As immigration in Wisconsin increased and spread across the state, many began to see that sources of information other than the local community and church were necessary. To meet this need the early immigrant press sought to reach and serve people not only in Wisconsin but also in settlements throughout the country. Attempting to be more than merely local newspapers, the news covered a wide range of intellectual and social concerns. Unlike the press in Norway, nearly all Norwegian-American newspapers remained very close to the grass roots. Their service was an immediate one: to inform those who could not as yet read the English language. In doing so they instructed their readers in the history and government of the United States, reported the news of Europe and Scandinavia, provided information concerning social and religious events, and kept the reader abreast of agricultural and business news.

The first Norwegian-American newspaper, *Nordlyset* (Northern Light), was established in Muskego in 1847. In its first issue the editors stated their intention: "Besides information about the constitution of this country and reports from Scandinavia, historical, agricultural, and religious news, we intend to bring contributions from private individuals and everything else that is suitable and useful for the information and entertainment of our readers. The editors will make every effort to preserve the strictest possible neutrality in matters of politics and religion." With this dictum the paper appeared regularly for three years, after which time the editors disbanded.

When *Nordlyset* ceased publication, other newspapers filled the vacuum. In the early 1850s the clergy began to take an interest in establishing a newspaper that would serve the interests of the emerging Norwegian Lutheran Church. Out of this desire came the *Emigranten* (The Emigrant). Founded by Reverend C. L. Clausen in 1852, this paper became an influential and long-lived pillar of Norwegian-American journalism.

Given the American system of government, the ethnic press found it impossible to remain politically neutral. Prior to any election many editors felt compelled to express their support for a local or national candidate. From its conception the *Emigranten* assumed an "independent Democratic" approach to state and local politics. Reflecting the views of the majority of its readers, it took a position against slavery, favored a liberal public land policy, and shared the hostile frontier attitude toward the land speculator.

As events in the 1850s led America closer to civil war, the *Emigranten*'s editorials dealt increasingly with the political issues of slavery and the preservation of the Union. The Republican party, with its strong stand against slavery and its promise of free land under the Homestead Act, began attracting the support of Norwegian voters. In 1857 the *Emigranten* cemented its stand on the issues by proclaiming "No Slavery for Black or White" and found itself rapidly moving to the Republican side.

Involved in American political and social events, the Norwegian-language press continued to fulfill various functions. While continuing to occupy much of its space with news from Norway and Europe, it also solicited accounts from Norwegian settlers in the new frontiers of the West and published several of the responses. Controversies of the day were aired, and one could always learn time and place of the various organization meetings in the news.

In the last quarter of the century many, especially those who had immigrated to America in the early periods, became concerned with the speed with which the newly arrived immigrants dropped their cultural traits. Dress, diet, language, economic success, in addition to the strong nativist pressure to conform, convinced the immigrants to modify their Norwegian customs and adopt American ways. In response to this influence, the ethnic press attempted to remind the immigrants to appreciate their own nationality. Printed in the pure Norwegian literary form, the press served as a cohesive force, setting up common interests among all the various Norwegian dialectal groups. In doing so, the ethnic press actively preserved the most important cultural trait of any group—its native language—and helped to make possible the boom in local and national societies that occurred around the turn of the century.

## FRONTIER AND FARM LIFE

In frontier Wisconsin, houses and barns by Norwegian immigrants often exhibited traditional architectural designs. Up until the time of the Civil War, log houses typified the dwellings in most settlement areas. In these early years many pioneers used the building techniques they had learned in Norway, especially in shaping and fitting logs and making corner notchings. In Scandinavia logs would often extend four or five inches past the corner, and the workmanship and ability of the builder could be gauged by how neatly he had finished these corners and the log ends. In America these techniques were modified, but builders continued to practice expert corner notching, fitting, and hewing of logs.

Immigrant farmers selected trees for their straightness and hand-hewed them with a broad axe. When laid upon one another, these shaped logs fitted together tightly. Because of the close fit, these log dwellings demanded only a minimal amount of chinking. Immigrant craftsmen painstakingly cut the log ends in dovetail fashion and joined them in a locking position with the ends directly above and below them. Frequently, Norwegians used wooden pins to ensure the stability of their log structure. Drilling vertical holes into two logs and joining them with a wooden pin insured the structure against warping. Gable ends were commonly logged up to the top. Lighter-weight logs (purlins) were placed horizontally along the length of the roof. Finally, builders nailed hand-split shingles or shakes to these purlins to complete the construction of the cabin.

In many cases, the immigrants replaced this cabin with another house of superior quality and comfort after a few years. The original log house then became useful as a workshop or summer kitchen. Norwegians, especially those settling in Wisconsin, often tended to build a number of outbuildings on their farms. This technique is associated with the traditional Norwegian system of agriculture called *Tun*. The clustering of small buildings, each serving a specific function, was common practice, since the remoteness of many regions of Norway demanded that farms act as self-sufficient units.

Norwegian farms in Wisconsin can be found with as many as sixteen small individual buildings, some of them serving a similar function as they would in Norway. A structure used exclusively for the storage of household items such as flour, flat bread, canning supplies, and clothes, for example, can often be found in a modified form on Norwegian-American farms. This building is referred to as a *Stabbur* in Norway and is distinctively Scandinavian. Another, called *eldhus*, or fire house, provided a place to bake flat bread, wash clothes, and heat water for butchering. Structures similar to those built by American farmers also appeared. These included, perhaps, a chicken coop, animal barn, feed storage barn, granary, workshop, water tower, and tobacco drying barn.

In the last third of the nineteenth century, distinctive Norwegian architectural traditions gradually fell into disuse. The introduction of the sawmill (which provided pre-cut timber) and advances in the field of construction methods (such as balloon framing) tended to Americanize Norwegian building techniques. After 1870 balloon frame barns could easily be built large enough to serve a number of different purposes. This new and more efficient American construction method made the Norwegian reliance on small outbuildings obsolete.

While the total number of Norwegian immigrants is small when compared to the total European immigration to the United States, no other country except Ireland contributed so great a percentage of its population to the United States. Between 1825 and 1915, no less than 750,000 Norwegians emigrated to America. Between 1838 and 1864 Wisconsin was the major focus of settlement. Including their American-born children, these pioneers probably contributed at least three million citizens to the United States.

Norwegians are one of the most ethnocentric immigrant groups in America, mainly because the Church and the ethnic press effectively struggled to preserve the Norwegian heritage. These institutions also stimulated the growth of Norwegian-American local and national societies. The *Bygdelag* movement (Old Home Society) is probably one of the most successful of these societies. Organized around the turn of the century, these clubs rapidly grew in popularity and represented the determination of Norwegian Americans to retain their ethnicity. As the historian Franklin C. Scott has written: "The Norwegian-Americans have been fortunate in that they have retained a profound love for the *fjords* and fields of the North while at the same time they have remained conscious of the fact that it was northern nature and economic conditions that impelled them to migrate. They loved their ancestral home in Norway, they took pride in their ancient heritage. Yet they recognized in America the chance for a better life and they appreciated that too."

Andreas Dahl Collection: PH 4255 (WHi D31 681), VMA

A Syttende Mai (May 17) celebration along the south shore of Lake Monona near Madison, mid-1870s. Syttende Mai, or Norwegian Constitution Day, celebrates the signing of the Norwegian constitution in 1814.

Courtesy Norskedalen Nature and Heritage Center

Coon Valley (Vernon County) tobacco growers display their product. Many Norwegian immigrants who originally settled in the Koshkonong area worked as agricultural laborers for the Yankee tobacco farmers of Dane County. As they moved west to areas like Coon Valley, they transplanted their newly acquired tobacco-growing skills. By 1880, Vernon County ranked fifth in the state in tobacco production.

Andreas Dahl Collection: PH 4255 (WHi D31 670), VMA

Lot 4973.2, VMA

*Both photos:* The dedication of East Blue Mounds Norwegian Lutheran Church, c. 1876. The dedication of a new church was both a celebration and a solemn occasion. Lutheran ministers sat front and center, as they often did in Norwegian communities in general.

Siri Rustebakke and her daughters and daughter-in-law work at carding and spinning at their Black Earth home, c. 1873.

The G. Thompson family, Cambridge.

Charles J. Van Schaick Collection: PH 3390 (WHi V22 1387), VMA

Maids in Black River Falls. Many single Norwegian immigrant women labored as domestic servants.

Andreas Dahl Collection: PH 4255 (WHi D31 606), VMA

Norwegian-American farmers inspect a plow at the Michelson plow shop, Argyle (Dane County), mid 1870s.

Name File, WHi(X3)34757

Halle Steensland (1832–1910) was born near Stavanger, Norway, and came to America in 1854. He became a prominent Madison businessman, philanthropist, and a leader of the state's Norwegian-American community. From 1872 to 1910 he served as vice-counsel for Sweden and Norway. Steensland's portrait, hanging on the back wall in this photo, is now displayed at the State Historical Society of Wisconsin.

Name File, WHi(X3)17587

Name File, WHi(X31)17358

Ole Evinrude (1877–1934) was born in Oslo, Norway, and grew up on a farm near Cambridge. He invented the outboard motor in 1910 and organized the Evinrude Motor Company, headquartered in Milwaukee.

After emigrating from Norway, Hjalmar Holand farmed near Ephraim. Holand wrote several histories about Norwegian Americans including *De norske settlementers historie* (The History of Norwegian Settlements) in 1908.

Frank Leslie's Illustrated Newspaper 4 April 1868, 44. WHi(X3)30252, VMA

*Top:* Ole Bull was an internationally famous Norwegian violinist whose American tours in the 1850s and 1860s drew huge crowds of Norwegian Americans. Here he is depicted arriving for a concert in Madison. Bull was not only a musical genius but also a utopian socialist. In 1870 Bull married Sarah Thorpe, the daughter of J. G. Thorpe, a wealthy Wisconsin lumberman. *Left:* Posters like this one advertised concerts by Anton O. Rundhaug of Perry Township (Dane County), who played the eight-string Norwegian violin at area functions in the early 1900s. *Below:* Note the two selections on the program composed by Ole Bull.

**PROGRAM:**

1. Longing for Home Composed by L. B. Fykerud
2. Christina Nelson's Memory
3. The Three Milk Maids on the Mountain
4. The Life of the Herdess Comp. by Ole Bull
5. The Water Falls Composed by Miller Boy
6. In My Father's Cabin Composed by Ole Bull
7. From the Cradle to the Grave
8. The Miller Boy's Masterpiece

Mount Horeb Area Historical Society

Andreas Dahl Collection: PH 4255  (WHi D353), VMA

The Fremad Läseselskabe Reading Society enjoyed an outing in the town of Moscow (Iowa County), October 9, 1875. This society testified to the literary interest among Norwegian immigrants.

Mount Horeb Area Historical Society

The Mount Horeb Lutheran Academy, sporting Norwegian flags, was dedicated on Syttende Mai, May 17, 1894. The Academy operated as a religious-based school following the tenets of the Lutheran Church. In 1903, the academy became a free high school.

Martha Gilbertson Mithus of Mount Horeb, c. 1900, wears a ceremonial Norwegian outfit, probably a wedding dress, complete with pins and crown.

*Tænk paa din skaber i din
ungdoms dage. Præd. 12, 1.*

## KARAKTERSEDDEL

Herved Bevidnes, at

*Carine Knudtson*

har besøgt religionsskolen i *Forward*

*skole Dist.*

i *20* dage og erholdt følgende karakter:

| | |
|---|---|
| Bibelhistorie | 70 |
| Forklaring | 95 |
| Kirkehistorie | — |
| Katekismus | — |
| Bibellæsning | 90 |
| Læsning | 95 |
| Grammatik *skrivning* | 90 |
| Diktat | 90 |
| Sang | 95 |
| Flid | 100 |
| Opförsel | 95 |

Alder: *14* aar. Skoletid: *34* dage.

*Perry* den *28 Sept 1908*

*Clara M. Daley*

LÆRER.

The report card of Norwegian American Carine Knudtson, received in the Forward School District, Perry Township (Dane County), 1908.

First Honors-Fall Festival -1927
Stoughton, Cambridge + Lodi, Wis.

PH 2361, WHi(X3)22817, VMA

The Sons of Norway, a large organization celebrating Norwegian heritage, has members throughout North America and in Norway. This local group displayed their ethnic pride on a float at a 1927 fall festival parade in Dane County.

Lot 1559, VMA

Gjertru Severson of Stoughton displayed her mastery of the traditional Norwegian craft of rosemaling.

# THE LETTERS OF OLE MUNCH RÆDER, 1847

*Ole Munch Ræder, a thirty-one-year-old scholar sent by the Norwegian govern-ment to study the American legal system, visited Wisconsin Territory in the fall of 1847 as part of a nationwide tour. On his journey, he visited Milwaukee, Madison, Jefferson, Janesville, and Elkorn and paid special attention to settlers from Norway. His letters describing the Norwegian community in Wisconsin were reprinted in newspapers in Norway and offered those back home another glimpse of life in America. In his letters, he wrestled with the strain felt by immigrants who wished to retain their ethnic identity while at the same time assimilate into a new society. We pick up his account as he is leaving Milwaukee. (From Gunnar J. Malmin, trans. and ed.,* America in the Forties: The Letters of Ole Munch Ræder *[Minneapolis: Norwegian-American Historical Association by the Uni-versity of Minnesota Press, 1929; copyright 1929, 1957 by University of Minne-sota], pp. 15–19, 37–43, 65–69. Breaks in the text are marked by ellipsis points.)*

. . . The next day, which was Sunday, a driver called for us in the morning with a coach drawn by two horses and, after a drive of a cou-ple of hours towards the southwest, we arrived at the Norwegian settle-ment at Muskego Lake. The first people whom we met were a couple from Tinn, both of whom seemed greatly pleased with the visit. True-hearted and simple, just as we find our countrymen here and there up among the mountains in Norway, they had preserved their customs, dress, and general arrangement of the house unchanged, as well as their language. They served us with excellent milk and whatever else they had; and, when they had become confident that we were altogether Norwegian, they also brought some excellent *flatbrød*, made of wheat, which they had at first held back because "these Yankees" are so ready to make fun of it. The Yankee who was with us, however, seemed very well pleased with it when we let him try it. On a later occasion we induced him to try another dish, just as Norwegian and just as unfamil-iar to him, namely, *fløtegrøt*, which he declared "first-rate" as he licked his lips. Our friends from Tinn were well satisfied with their condition; they had managed so well during the first four years that they had paid off the debt that they had incurred and now they already had a little surplus.

We next visited, among others, Even Heg, who seems to be one of the leaders among the Norwegians in these parts. He is said to be a Haugean and he was away attending a devotional meeting when we reached his house. He, too, seemed satisfied with the state of his affairs. He did not feel very friendly towards Reiersen, who, in his opinion, had given exaggerated accounts of the unhealthful conditions at Muskego and had thereby frightened the later Norwegian immigrants to such an extent that they not only would not settle there but they even went miles out of their way to avoid going through the place. Mr. Heg, by the way, has earned the gratitude of the Norwegians in Wisconsin by starting a printing establishment on his own farm, with the assistance of Mr. Bache, a financier from Drammen, who lives with him. Here they publish the Norwegian-Wisconsin newspaper, *Nordlyset*, edited by Mr. Reymert. It is without doubt a very good idea through such a medium to maintain a cultural link between the Norwegians here and the mother country, as well as among themselves. Every one, indeed, who would like to see them preserve their national characteristics and their memories of their native land as long as possible must, first and foremost, turn his attention to the problem of preserving their language by keeping it constantly before their eyes and ears.

As you know, I cannot convince myself that all these countrymen of ours, as they leave our own country, are to be regarded as completely lost and as strangers to us. On the contrary, I believe that they are carrying on a great national mission—in accordance with the wishes of Providence, working through their instinctive desire to wander. Their mission consists in proclaiming to the world that the people of the Scandinavian countries, who in former days steered their course over every sea and even found their way to the distant shores of Vinland and Hvidmanna-land, have not been blotted out from among the peoples of the earth, nor have they degenerated. After having regained their independence, so that they can show themselves in the world, they come to demand their place in that country upon which their fathers cast the first ray of light, no matter how flickering and uncertain, and to take part in the great future which is in store for this youthful, but already mighty, republic. Let them become Americans, as is the duty of holders of American soil, but this need not prevent them from remaining Norwegian for a long time to come. The American character is not yet so fixed and established that it excludes all others. The Americans are satisfied with

demanding a few general traits of political rather than of really national significance. Under such lenient influences, the aliens are elevated
and improved, rather than changed; they lose their sharp edges and
adopt some of the good qualities of others. Even if America, fulfilling
also in this respect a great and providential purpose, shall in the end
absorb and mold together into a compact whole all the various nationalities which now are making their contributions in such rich measure,
and shall not only blot out the many prejudices which now separate people in their home countries but also absorb some of the individual characteristics which now constitute the peculiar qualities of each nation,
even if such be the case, then surely it will be for us, as well as for every
other European nation, not merely a source of satisfaction as an historical fact, but perhaps also, in the course of events, a factor of real benefit
that our Scandinavian North has become one of the parent nations for
this nation to whose lot will undoubtedly some day fall the place of lead-
ership in the affairs of the world. . . .

The ease with which the Norwegians learn the English language has
attracted the attention of the Americans, all the more because of the
fact that they are altogether too ready to consider them entirely raw
when they come here. "Never," one of them told me a few days ago,
"have I known people to become civilized so rapidly as your countrymen; they come here in motley crowds, dressed up with all kinds of din-
gle-dangle just like the Indians. But just look at them a year later: they
speak English perfectly, and, as far as dress, manners, and ability are
concerned, they are quite above reproach." Of course I tried to explain
to him that their original mode of dress certainly could not make Indians out of them and that they were not entirely devoid of culture or
those habits of diligence and regularity which one expects to find in a
well-ordered and civilized society, even among the poorest classes out in
the country, but he seemed scarcely disposed to make any concessions
on that point.

On the other hand, he did not seem to know a great deal about the
Norwegians in this country. My impression, after many visits extending
over a number of settlements, is that the great mass of the families have
essentially changed very little. I shall not deny, however, that they have
been able to meet the severe strain of the work with an iron will, and
thus have had ample opportunity to strengthen their moral courage, and
it also seems to be a fact that there is less drinking here than in Norway,

although there are enough drunkards here, too, and among them some who have acquired the habit since they came here. Cleanliness is, here as in Norway, for many of them almost an unheard-of thing. The entrance to one of the houses I visited was guarded by a formidable cesspool. If a place looks really filthy and disreputable, you must expect to meet either Norwegians or Swiss or Irish ("Eirisa," as the Norwegians call them).

Of course there are some notable exceptions, but, on the whole, one must admit that it is particularly among young people who have gone into the service of Americans that one finds a real desire for improvement. This it is which makes the Norwegian name respected and almost loved here. This it is which has given our people such a general reputation for respectability, morality, sobriety, and natural ability that I frequently hear expressions to the effect that the whole of Norway might well come here and be received with open arms. On account of these qualities Norwegian young people are much in demand as servants. I believe there is not a single house of any size at all in Madison where Norwegians are not found. Here at the American Hotel, where I am staying, all the female servants are Norwegians. One of them, a woman, whose children are at Koshkonong, does not yet now the language and consequently she receives less than she otherwise could earn; her pay is a dollar a week. The same wage is paid to a young girl who knows the language only slightly. A girl who is a sister of a clerk in Christiania has just recently come to this country and she is paid seventy-five cents. The hostler is also Norwegian and receives twelve dollars a month. The first day I was here a Norwegian boy, fourteen or fifteen years old, waited on table; when I asked him his wages he answered that he was paid only five dollars a month. I thought he expressed himself that way with a secret feeling of triumph, to give me a real surprise, but soon afterwards he proved that he meant what he said quite literally by finding a better job elsewhere. My host said he was sorry to see him leave.

A few weeks ago I found three Norwegians in consultation outside the door to my hotel. One of them had tentatively hired himself out to a man living a few miles from here, for whom my host functions as a sort of agent. He was to try the job for a month at five dollars and, after that, if both parties were satisfied, he was promised better pay. Now, however, the boy had found better employment here in Madison and he wished to substitute another in his place, a boy from Bergen who had just arrived. The third, who to function in the capacity of interpreter for them, did not feel himself quite competent for the task and was greatly pleased to have me relieve him. We got hold of Mr. Morrison my host, who did not object very much, although the new man was very young and so short of stature that the Yankee suspected that he might be a Lapp. I reassured him, however, and our good countryman was soon sent on his way, with a good breakfast in his stomach and a lunch in his pocket.

You see, therefore, that five dollars is somewhat below the average monthly wage in the country and is paid only at the very start when the worker is on trial; afterwards the pay is increased considerably, at least to twelve dollars, I believe. One who hires himself out by the day to cut or bind grain during the harvest season can earn as much as dollar a day, in addition to his board. A simple laborer at the lead mines earns from ten to twelve dollars a month and board. A tender at a tile factory told me he made eleven dollars a month. These wages are not, however, as a rule paid entirely in cash; some part, ordinarily half, is paid in goods. Girls, naturally, are paid less, both in the towns and in the country. One with whom I spoke at a restaurant some miles east of Madison was paid a dollar and a quarter per week; she knew the language. The highest wages I have heard of for women is seven dollars a month; the favored individual is a beautiful young girl at a hotel here in Madison; I believe she is regarded as a lady in the social life here.

It is, on the whole, quite remarkable how quickly our farm-girls improve when they are out among strangers. Their English is quite correct, but as soon as they start to speak their mother tongue, it generally sounds broad and clumsy enough; no matter how much patriotic love you may profess to feel for the various dialects of our language, you cannot deny or at any rate avoid the feeling that the harmony is broken, even if the unfortunate expression comes from the fairest mouth or is animated by the friendliest smile. I believe that most of them are not conscious of the peculiar impression made by their way of speaking Norwegian; at any rate, they are too good-hearted and too happy in the recollection of their native land to be bothered by such a trifle. One can scarcely say as much for the Norwegian boys; at any rate, I have heard the opinion expressed that as soon as they have learned "to guess" and "to calculate," they at once become strangers to their less fortunate countrymen and are very loath to admit their Norwegian origin. This fact (and I am inclined to believe it is one) furnishes new proof of the need of improving the cultural conditions among our countrymen here and, at the same time, of increasing their national pride so much, at least, that they will not feel themselves tempted to deny their own country. I do not believe that any cultured Norwegian has ever felt any tendency to do such a thing; on the contrary he is all too apt to boast of the fact that he comes from the "land of the heroes." He realizes, at any rate, that his country, in spite of its poverty, has every claim to the respect of strangers; and he will not so easily be overwhelmed by the feeling of reverence for "these mighty Yankees," which seems to affect our simple countrymen so deeply and probably accounts for the fact that they make such good servants, much better, in fact, than they were in their own country. If this reverence could only reduce itself to a feeling of respect for the enterprise and other good qualities of the Yankees, then their desire to progress, instead of being mere servile imitation, would assume a somewhat more honorable aspect. Thus, instead of trying to lose themselves among the mass of strangers, as Jews do when they are converted, they would continue their relations with their countrymen, on whom they could thus exert a most beneficial influence.

They have all the more reason for assuming such an attitude because of the fact, as already indicated, that the Americans themselves certainly do not consider it a disgrace to be Norwegian. It cannot, of course, be said that they have any particular respect for the culture of the Norwegians or for their spirit of independence, a thing which is here considered of great importance as a civic virtue, because the sort of intelligence which is shown in a more or less successful attempt at imitation is always of a somewhat lower type. But as soon as the young people have risen from their present status as servants and have become independent farmers or shop-owners, and that time is not so far distant, then the Norwegians will without doubt enjoy the respect and confidence of their fellow-citizens, which will show itself through election to public offices—provided that they do not forfeit this good will by their own actions. . . .

I must add that, among all the people I have talked with—and they are not a few—I have found very few who said they were dissatisfied and wanted to return to Norway, and with some of these it was more a matter of talk than of a real desire to go. One man said he wanted to return home because his wife did not like it here; another, who said he was a

Quaker, was dissatisfied with the schools. Both of them had been talking in this vein for a long time, without making any real move in that direction but rather the opposite. A little merchant from Drammen, on the other hand, seemed to mean it seriously; he has been rather unfortunate, for which I am sorry, as he seems to be a very fine man. And it is not strange if there are some who have been ruined through their emigration. The emigration fever spread through our country districts like a disease, paying no heed to age or sex, rich or poor, the diligent worker or the lazy good-for-nothing. Naturally, many have emigrated who are totally unfit for the strenuous life here, which demands so much energy, common sense, and endurance if one is to succeed. It is equally true that many have made a mistake in buying or claiming land before they had either the necessary understanding or means to proceed with its cultivation. The fact that there have not been more wrecks than there have, in view of all the mistakes made, gives evidence both of the inherent strength of character of our people and of the excellence of the country itself.

I do not mean to imply that few complaints are heard. Quite the contrary. In addition to the fact that many, indeed most, admit that they had expected the land to be far better than it actually proved to be and that they had been fooled, to some extent, by the false reports contained in letters, there are many other complaints; but all of them are of such a nature that time and habit will presumably remedy the situation. Some complain that the work is too strenuous, others that there is so much ungodliness, others that there is too much sickness. One woman complained that there seemed to be less real nourishment in the food here than in Norway; no matter how much good food she gave her husband, he simply would not gain in weight. Possibly, she thought, and very likely with good reason, this was due to the severe heat which, coupled with strenuous labor, sapped his energy.

Practically all the Norwegians have been sick, some of them as much as a year at a time, and this misfortune has hampered many. When I told a group of Norwegians at Muskego that Mr. Fribert had written a book in which he says that Wisconsin is one of the most healthful places on earth, they all laughed; yet Fribert's opinion coincides with that of American physicians, and, indeed, it is put down as an indisputable fact in books, papers, and official documents. It is included as a standing expression in all official speeches and as the fairest rose in the rhetorical bouquet which the governor presents to his legislature at the opening of its annual session. It is not even conceded that, as in every newly settled country, there is naturally a great deal of sickness which will gradually disappear. Such sickness, they say, is caused by the cutting away of the woods; the vegetable matters which covers the ground is thus exposed to sun and winded, its decomposition is quickened and the air becomes polluted. But, in Wisconsin, they say, there are woods only in small parts of the state, most which consists of open prairies that of course do not have to be cleared.

In answer to this argument I merely point to the daily newspapers, which are half filled with all kinds of quack advertisements of pills and marvelous medicines against fever and ague and bilious fever, and to a certain Dr. Champion, who drove by here most ostentatiously the other day with two huge boxes of pills. I do not believe there is any other country on earth where sound, healthy people use as much medicine as here, for the prevention of disease. But, of course, you may say that there is sickness in every country, Norway included. "We carry on the sale of pills, as we do everything else here, on a large scale," it is said: and of course, every man is entitled to his own opinion. Still it is a fact that many people have suffered much from these fevers, especially the immigrants. Last fall was particularly bad in this respect, as the heat had been oppressive. This year the situation is not quite so bad. I have been in the best of health, with the exception of a few days, in spite of the abrupt changes from hot to cold weather which we have had and which are said to have been particularly severe this year. Many complain of the sudden change from the severely cold winter to the hot summer, a condition which is said to prevail in most parts of America; for example, in New York the winter is said to be as cold as in Christiania and the summer as hot as in Naples; I do not know how much truth there is in that.

Some complain that the thunderstorms and other natural phenomena here are so violent that the uninitiated become thoroughly alarmed. A Norwegian family found it so terrifying at first to see "the heavens in a blaze" that they crept into a cellar. It is true that the thunder rumbles with great majesty here and that the lightning flashes across the heavens in a particularly lively fashion, when a storm is given free rein, and that happens often.

The worst complaint of all is homesickness; everyone experiences that, of course. But time can heal even deeper wounds than that of having been severed from one's native land. Furthermore, most of the immigrants seem to cherish more or less consciously a hope of returning some day to their native land, having realized only after they had broken away how strong were the ties that held them there.

In addition to all these troubles and complaints, I found, particularly among those who had owned a considerable property in Norway, a quite general feeling of satisfaction that they had come, built rather on their hopes for the future, to be sure, than on what they had already achieve. Among those who have worked their way up from poverty this feeling of satisfaction is so great that they are likely to overestimate their present prosperity. A certain Lars Hedemarken (or Rollo, after the farm by that name in Ringsake) is now a well-to-do man and is highly esteemed for his uprightness. I mentioned one of the largest farms in Ringsaker and asked him how he would like to trade his present farm for that one. He said he would not do so under any circumstances, chiefly because the farm in Ringsaker would prove far too small for all his sons, where here the whole prairie was theirs. His house was one of the better kind. Very few Norwegians have yet built comfortable houses. The great majority live in log cabins of the sort that can be erected in a day.

You will probably ask if I found anything that would indicate that dissatisfaction with political conditions in Norway had influenced anyone to emigrate; in Norway, as you know, there has been considerable loose talk to this effect. Of course I could not very well ask people bluntly for fear that they might suspect me of being some sort of inquisitor. Nevertheless I gave them all an opportunity to express themselves on this question by asking them their motives for emigrating. All except one, who said he had religious grounds, spoke of economic motives, of the hope that their children would have a better future here, and so forth. Only two people remarked casually that people in Norway did not enjoy so great a degree of freedom. I asked one of them if he did not think that the people are their own masters and lawmakers in Norway also, but he answered that this was only on paper. "A person there isn't even master of his own body"—which, however, could as well be said of people here in America. The same man expressed his satisfaction with economic conditions, by saying, "Here even a tramp can enjoy a chicken dinner once in a while.". . .

# THE LETTERS OF ANDERS JENSEN STORTROEN, 1857–1862

*The letters of Anders Jensen Stortroen offer a different perspective of the Norwegian immigrant experience from Ole Munch Ræder's narrative printed above. Ræder writes as a scholar seeking to describe with accuracy the early stages of Norwegian settlement in Wisconsin. Stortroen, an immigrant writing to his family in Tönset, Norway, offers a less analytic but more textured account of the struggles and accomplishments of an immigrant to Wisconsin. While Ræder described life in southern Wisconsin in the year prior to statehood, Stortroen usually writes from northwestern Wisconsin and from more than two decades after the first Norwegians settled in the state. The text that appears here was translated from the Norwegian by Paul Bjerkeng of Milwaukee and is reprinted from* The Wisconsin Magazine of History *in 1931 (vol. 15, 356–369). The original manuscripts are held by the Pierce County Historical Association.*

*In the opening letter of September 1857, Stortroen describes the ocean voyage from Norway and the overland trip to Black Earth in south central Wisconsin. A year later, Stortroen had settled in Martell Township in northwestern Wisconsin and was writing from the home of Karl Olsen Bergebakken, a Norwegian settler. Stortroen's growing prosperity is evident in the final two letters written from his farm in Pierce County. During the four and a half years covered by these letters, Stortroen had purchased more than 160 acres of land, married, and built a home and barn. Together, the letters reflect the various stages of the immigrant experience as lived by many Norwegians who came to Wisconsin.*

Written Sept. 27th, 1857

Dear Parents, Brothers and Sisters!

Since our wish has been fulfilled, and we have arrived at Hans Christoffersen's, through many troubles, to remain here this winter, we will not neglect to tell you of our experiences on this journey to America.

We left Drammen July 8th, and passed by the last shore of Norway, called Lillesund, on the 14th. The 22nd we saw Scotland, and sailed by. We did not see England, as we passed to the north of it, namely on the North Sea. The 21st of August we saw the first coasts of America, called the Newfoundland Islands.

The 3rd of September we came to an island, 6 miles from Quebec, where we landed and washed clothes. On the 6th we left and came to Quebec on the 7th. On the 9th we left Quebec, boarded a steamer, and came to Montreal on the 10th. We left there at once on another steamer and came to Kingston on the 12th, left there at once and came to Hamilton on the 13th where we took a train; we reached Detroit on the 14th, where we changed trains, leaving at once for Chicago where we arrived the same day.

We boarded a steamer the same evening and came to Milwaukee on the 15th. The trip to Milwaukee cost $10.00 each, children from 3 to 12 years paying half fare. The Captain had made this bargain for us while we were yet on board ship, for we sailed on the English line. We likewise had a free interpreter to that place.

On the 15th we left Milwaukee, and reached Blekker[1] on the evening of the same day. That cost $3.50 apiece. We rested there at the homes of some Norwegians from Valders. Then Ole (Stortroen) and I left to hunt up Hans C (Tröan) while Paul (Bjerkeng) and his family remained there. Ole E had remained at the hospital on the island where we washed clothes, because his two youngest children were sick. And while in Chicago, Tollof and Lars took another route to Iowa, because they had borrowed money from two Telemarken boys, and therefore had to accompany them.

We hired a guide on the 17th, when we left Blekker; he accompanied us about 14 miles, and on the 18th we hired another, but he took a wrong road, so we went 22 miles out of our way. We asked the name (Hans C) of all the Norwegians we met, but none knew him. But as luck would have it, we met a Norwegian, who told us we were on the wrong road. The reason was that the fog was so thick that day, we went east instead of southwest. So we turned around, while the guide went directly on to the nearest town. We retraced our route, very apprehensive, but providentially we reached the home of a Norwegian where Hans had stayed one winter, and were well informed as to where he was. Very happy and satisfied, we rested there until the next day, when we got him to accompany us directly to Hans, who lived about 10 miles from there. This was on September 19th.

---

1 Probably Black Earth, the nearest railway station to some of the Norwegian settlements in western Dane County.

On the 20th Hans and I went to Blekker to get our baggage and
Paul and his family, while Ole remained. We came from there on the
22nd to Hans', where we are now.

According to our promise, we will inform you about the storms we
encountered while on the ocean, as we noted down every time. On the
night of July 31st there was a terrible storm, so that for our part we were
certain that the waves would engulf us, had not the power of the
Almighty been greater. We were on the ocean for 8 weeks, and perhaps
the following also belongs in this letter. We were in number 277 passengers on this ship when we left, but the Lord took pleasure in calling to
himself by death 8 souls of our company, of which 2 were adults and 6
children.

We should perhaps give you a little information concerning conditions in this country, although we ourselves have not had much experience in that respect. But we dare confidently affirm that there is a great
deal of difference between the customs and profits here in America and
in Norway. As proof of this, we will tell you in this letter how much
Hans has prospered in 2 years. When we reached his place, he had 8
oxen, 3 cows, 1 heifer, 14 hogs, of which 6 will be butchered this fall, and
20 hens. Likewise 80 acres of land.

He has acquired this inside of two years, because he was sick for half
a year before that, costing him what he had earned before that. But you
must know that he has worked diligently, late and early, and has used his
wits in planning in the best possible manner. He will not sell his property now for less than $1000.00. But there are taxes and expenses here as
well as in Norway, though not as large. Now that we have in the course
of many arguments found out a great deal, we will advise you, that you
may know it likewise. The milk here is just as good as in Norway, and all
kinds of foods are as good, there need be no doubt of it. By no means
will we advise anyone to come over here, but you must advise yourselves
concerning this, since there are many hard paths and many tribulations
to endure that one cannot understand before he starts out.

We have, God be praised, good health after this journey, and we
cannot complain of a single day's sickness after we left you. At least we
did not suffer in the least from seasickness, although there were but 9 or
10 of us who were well; the others vomited and were very sick.

We will break short our poor and incomplete letter with hearty
greetings to you all. Please greet all acquaintances and relatives who

enquire after us. If any one should have an inclination to follow us to American, inform us definitely of it in advance.

In closing, may the peace and blessing of the Lord be with us and with you in this life; but above all, when we shall make our last journey from this vale of sorrow, may we meet with joy before God, where there is no more sorrow or separation. Parents, brothers and sisters are diligently greeted from your devoted sons and brothers.

Anders Jensen (Stortroen)

❧

[Martell Township, Wisconsin
Fall 1858]

Since we have been in America about ten months, and have traveled extensively both in Illinois, and now in different places in Wisconsin, we will this time give you as exact information as possible as to how America really is, and also concerning conditions here, as accurately as we have discovered them to be in every particular at these places. You must excuse us for not having fully informed you about this before, but we have not had any actual experience, and did not want to write what others have told us. It is hard for one here in America to write a letter to you in Norway and take the responsibility for having written too much or too little, but put it down exactly as it is here, because if any of you should get the desire to follow us to America on account of these letters, and they did not describe conditions as they are here, we would consider ourselves unfortunate in that we have led anyone astray. But we will describe things in this letter as accurately as possible and as we understand them, then each and every one must do as they like, whether they wish to come to America or not.

We will first tell you about the country, and we can say at once that it is a very fertile land, as one can sow almost what kind of seed he chooses, and he will be certain that it comes up, and just as certain that it will not freeze down again. Neither is there any trouble with fertilizing for any type of farming, as it is unnecessary. Here the land is uniformly level except for small hills and valleys, so one place looks like another wherever one goes. In this locality the water is just as wholesome and good as in Norway, there being no difference. But as far as the woods are concerned, they are unpraiseworthy, since here no trees but oaks can be found, and they are not very plentiful on the farms the Norwegians have bought lately; but some of the Americans who settled here first have much woods and of the best quality, and they naturally did not settle in the poorest places. For they found both the most convenient locations and the best forests.

Their meadows consist of prairies and sloughs. Prairies are large level stretches where one cannot see forests in any direction while standing in the midst of the prairies, but can see only the blue rim of the sky around. And the sloughs are like the marshes in Norway as they are on wet land. And both kinds of meadows bear large crops, yes, fully as large as the luxuriant grass in Norway. Still, some of the Americans broke up land and seeded timothy seed which gives extremely high yields, and which is the best and most nourishing hay crop here also. What we call a "gaard" in Norway is called a farm here, and a large farm here consists of a dwelling house, a cellar and a stable. And here can be found many who have lived in America three or four years who do not yet have any house but live in cellars dug out of the ground. Fine houses are built mostly of timbers (logs), but they do not bevel the logs here as in Norway, but they let the logs lie as they first fall, then they take stones or whatever is most convenient and chink between the logs, later working together clay and lime and plastering the walls, and with that they are ready. And the roofs of the houses are of boards, since here neither birch bark, sod or stone (slate) are used for roofs. Some of the Americans have houses which are built of sawed lumber, which are large and fine. (There are enough buildings here after a fashion (if one could only thrive in such, which is the most difficult for all who come here).)

The winters here are neither as long or as cold as in Norway, and houses are needed for neither wheat or corn, as they make a box of boards in the field to put the crop in, cover it with straw for a roof, where it can stand until they haul it away and sell it. They haul their hay together and put it in stacks near their stables-those who have stables, otherwise a large number of the cattle spend the winter in the open.

The Norwegian farmers here have generally from 80 to 160 acres land, and an acre consists of about three Norse "maal." This is all their property, where they have their fields, their meadows and their pastures, likewise their woods, which will hardly suffice for many, to furnish enough building material, fuel and fences. From 10 to 40 acres of each farm have been cleared and put under cultivation, according to means.

And the cultivated land is used to raise all kinds of crops.

On this much land one can live very peacably and comfortably when he is not in debt. It is not much better to be debt here than in Norway. For from 10 to 30 per cent interest is charged here, and summons and auctions occur here as well as in Norway. There are taxes and expenses for the farmer here as in Norway, although not as large. As far as earnings are concerned, there is a great deal of difference between here and Norway, since here a common laborer gets from 50c to $1.50 per day at this time,-it differs with the different kind of work and the hours are from six or seven a.m. to seven or eight p.m. the year around, as the days here are almost the same length all the time, and the nights are as dark the year around as they are in the fall over there.

There has been a serious financial depression here this year, as the wheat has been very cheap so wages have been generally lower than usual. There is better pay here for any kind of an artisan than for a common laborer; (although we have not worked at our trade for others very much, but have done only what was needed for ourselves, because) but one must learn to speak English well before one can carry on competently as a craftsman.

Here may be found all sorts of animals and creatures, both tame and wild animals. The tame animals are generally larger than in Norway; but the wild animals are smaller. Two horses here, six or seven years old cost from $250 to $300; two oxen four or five years old cost from $70 to $100; a cow from $20 to $30, and the cows milk a little more here than in Norway as a rule, and the milk is also just as good here as there. A four-wheeled wagon costs from $70 to $90, a plow costs from $12 to $18, a harrow from $4 to $8. A bushel wheat costs 50 cents, a bushel corn (maize) 25 cents, a bushel oats 15 cents, a bushel potatoes 12$\frac{1}{2}$ cents. We have not seen rye or barley here.

One pound butter costs 10 cents, one pound pork 8 cents, one pound coffee 16 cents, one pound sugar 16 cents, one pound tobacco 40 cents, a pot of whiskey 12 cents. But both weights and measures are smaller here than in Norway, and prices vary here just like there. Clothing is much more expensive here than there. A pair of boots costs $5, a pair of shoes $2, one pair of trousers of wool and cotton cloth $3, a coat of the same cloth $5. More need not be mentioned.

We will tell you a little about religion which may cause you to reflect, when you hear how different it is in this part of the world in that respect. There are many different religions here, and one has the opportunity to embrace which ever one he chooses. One can hear a preacher here six times a year at most when one is in the vicinity, although we have not heard a minister preach more than two times since we were in Norway, as we have been absent on journeys. Religious services are held at the homes of the farmers in turn, as they do not have a church here, although we have seen several churches around here. But there is talk of building a church here also, in time, as they have fenced in a church yard this summer and have already dedicated it, so in time it will be a little more cheerful in that respect.

Here are also Norwegian schools (though not arranged like those in Norway) so those who want to educate their children and bring them up in a God-fearing manner have the opportunity to do so; but here are found many of those who are so indifferent that they attend neither religious services or school, as there is no compulsion in such cases. Still, one can lead as Christian a life here as in Norway if he chooses to do so (although it is really more difficult).

There are many, entirely too many temptations here, and many tempters who will lead one astray. On the other hand, there are few counselors here in America to comfort and guide one on the path which leads to Eternal Life and Salvation, as compared with where you are. And we will remind you, relatives and acquaintances at Faaset, that if any of you should desire to come to America, do not delude yourselves into the belief that you will hear as many good admonitions as you have heard, and will hear, at Faaset, for you will surely miss them.

As concerns the weather, there has been an excessive amount of rain and thunder this spring and summer, so no one can remember the like of it. Likewise, the heat was so intense the last part of June, that it was almost impossible to work at all. If we sat down in the shade, the sweat drops ran off our clothes like hail, and we had to change shirts two and three times each day. One can not work outside in the rain here, either, for it will bring on illness; so you must not estimate earnings for each day here.

For the sake of room we must close our humble letter although we have not written one tenth of what we would say had we been there. But a word more: that there is a great deal of difference, both in mode of living and profits, compared to Norway, you may be sure of, if one only can thrive here.

Anders Jensen Stortroen

Written January 13th, 1861

You must pardon us for letting such a long time elapse before answering your last letter, which was dated April 6th, and reached us May 8th last year. One reason for this was that we wanted to wait until after harvest and threshing, so we would know how much we raised on the farm we worked this past year, as well as a few other news items we will tell about.

We got 200 bushels of wheat and 104 bushels of oats for our share. We also had four acres of corn, but that was destroyed when it was sprouting by an animal which is called a gopher here, which resembles the water-rat in Norway, so we had nothing for our work. Nevertheless we can say we have done well, as it was a pretty good year, and the prices for the crops fair; wheat is 62 cents a bushel now, and oats are 25 cents. We made about a dollar a day for the time we worked with it.

We can inform you that we have built a house and a barn since we last wrote. We built our house last spring, and were kept busy a long time, as it is large compared with such dwelling houses here in America. It is 16 ells (32 feet) long and 10 ells (20 feet) wide, inside measure, and two full stories high. The timbers are hewed of oak and also beveled, so it was a lot of work and it took a long time to erect. We have divided it in tow, as the whole room would be too large for so few people to live in. We built our barn last fall, and moved to our home November 1st. We cannot take credit to ourselves for laying aside much money this year, as it costs a lot to build, and there are many other expenses when one takes up his residence here in America, as everything is expensive. We have only two cows, two calves a year old, and three hogs, to date.

We have had a very nice winter so far. Five weeks before Christmas we got a foot of snow, and it has not been very cold since, but quite mild. Earnings are a little better than last year, although the scarcity of money continues, but it is to be hoped that if the coming year will be as good as the past, times will improve.

You will be glad to hear that we have all our usual health. We are asked to greet you all from Paul Bjerkeng and his family, likewise from old Nils Nilsen Neby and his family, and tell you that they are all well. We hope you will write to us as soon as you get this letter and tell us in detail of all the events which have occurred in the neighborhood. Especially we would like to hear how Lars Jordet is, as he has been continually in our thoughts since we heard he was sick, and you must greet him diligently from us, if he is still alive. Greet all relatives and friends from us, tell them we would like it very much if any of our acquaintances should wish to follow us to this country.

We can also tell you that Peder Hektoen was up here for a three weeks visit, and he is enjoying good health and prosperity. We heard from Ole Faadal a month ago; he and his family are all well, and he had decided to move up here next spring. But we have not had any letters from Tollof of Lars Moen since last winter.

Ole can tell you that he shot a deer with the rifle we took along, shortly before Christmas. He shot it a short distance away from our home. There is an abundance of game around here, but time is too short to hunt very much, and it does not pay to do too much of that kind of work. Last fall we also did some fishing in a small stream (Rush River) which flows about an English mile from here. We used a net we had made. The fish were trout just like in the brooks in Norway, and we could have caught a lot if we had time and better equipment to catch the fish with.

As we do not recall anything else of importance to write about now, we sincerely hope that these poor lines will find you well, and we pray from our hearts to the Compassionate and Merciful God that He will keep and protect both you and us with His gracious Care and Blessing through the dangerous wilderness of this world. And we ask you all not to forget to pray for us when you pray for yourselves, as we who are so far, far off from Father and Mother, from Sister and Brother, will not forget to do for you. And then we will in happy expectation, hope and believe that if not before, which is uncertain, then after resurrection we may meet on the other side of the grave, where there is no more separation, but can live together throughout Eternity.

In closing dear Parents and Sisters and Brothers, you are given a heartfelt and loving greeting from your devoted sons and brothers, and we wish you a Happy and Joyful New Year.

Your sincere and faithful sons and brothers,
Anders and Ole Jensen Stortroen

Stortroen in Pierce County, Wisconsin
January 1862

Dear parents, brothers and sisters!

Since we have for a long time been thinking of writing a letter to you, we must make an effort to do so. The reason for this delay was that Paul Bjerkeng has been waiting for a long time for an answer to the letter he sent to Norway last spring and which was addressed to his father at Bjerkeng. Since this has not come, we cannot keep you in ignorance about whether we are alive yet or not.

Your letter dated March 15th last winter arrived the first of May, and we were not only very glad to hear that our beloved parents and brothers and sisters were in good health and well in every respect, but also that other relatives and acquaintances were as usual. It may be hard for you, dear parents and brethren, to realize how welcome each word in your letters to us is, which tells about conditions and circumstances there, as you might know that we who were brought up there, and remember former conditions well, delight greatly in hearing how present conditions are everywhere. We have heard reports from other letters from that vicinity, of news (which we do not know whether to believe or not, since you did not mention them), not of any consequence, but nevertheless of interest to us. For example, that Anders Husan is married; that old Esten Losegaard and old Iver Oien are dead, and other local news of like character. Please be so good as to tell us a little more news like this in your next letter.

Again we can, to God alone belongs the Praise and Glory for it, give you the glad new, that we are enjoying continued good health and prosperity. You might like to hear how times are here and what we have been doing since we last wrote to you. Last winter we worked a little on our own land, and in between times I made shoes and Ole did some tailoring. Last spring we worked out almost all the time. We did mostly carpenter work. At first we worked by the day, and then we got 75 cents per day. Then we contracted to build a stable for a man, for which we received 22 dollars, and as it took us 11 days, we got one dollar per day. During harvest we worked out also, as we do not have any wheat yet, but harvest lasted only nine days and then we earned $1.50 per day each.

After harvest last fall we contracted to build a house, and Thore Bersvensen Bruen from Tyldal was with us, so we were three on that contract. We were to build it of hewed timbers for $60, and we made fairly well by it as we averaged a dollar a day each. The house was 14 ells long (28 feet) and 10 ells wide (20 feet) and two full stories. We hewed the logs, which were of oak, on the ground before we hauled them up in place, but we did not bevel them as he did not wish to have the logs lie to close together. There has been a lot of building done here lately, as the houses have been poor, and there were very few who could do such work before we came; neither have people had as food incomes before as they now are beginning to have.

Last year was poor as far as crops were concerned, as they go only 15 bushels wheat per acre where they got 30 the summer before, and that was small and poor wheat; but corn and potatoes and other such crops were a little better. We had also a very nice fall here. We got about six inches of snow about a month before Christmas, and ever since we have had fine, mild weather.

You have doubtless seen in the newspapers or heard through letters about the great war here in America, which is the reason for scarcity of money here. It is said that the reason this war started was that when they last had a presidential election, the Southern states chose a Democrat and the Northern states a Republican. The Northern states had a majority of the votes, and their Republican became president. The Southerners became so embittered they elected their own president, and started a war to chastise the Northerners; for the Northern states are free, and the Southern states are slave states. We are not well-informed enough to judge which of these are right. We and most of the Norwegians around here voted for the Southern Democrat for president, however.

There have been many battles now, a battle being fought almost daily, and many have fallen on both sides. But according to the papers and letters received here from the front, Southern losses have been greatest. It is 800 or 900 miles from our home to the nearest front or battlefield. Men enlist (or hire out) for this war, but most people think they can hardly conscript anyone, since it is a civil war. A married man or one with a family gets $13 a month and a bonus of $100 when the war is over. His wife or his family gets $5 a month from the county and $5 from the state as long as he is in service, and if he falls his wife or family gets a pension. But a single man gets $13 a month and is promised $100 when the war is over. There are many from here who have gone to war, both Norwegians and other nationalities. The Northern army is said to number 700,000 men, and they have hardly any knowledge of how large the Southern army is, so they are probably the largest armies the world has ever seen. We hope and pray to the Merciful God, the Ruler of all things, that He will soon end this strife, or the times will be hard and it will be difficult to live here in America.

Last winter, on March 25th, we bought 160 acres land from the government which lies alongside what we already had. Such land may be bought on the condition that inside of 30 days from the time you buy it and get the first papers, which cost $2, you must build a house and live there. There is not much land like that left now which is conveniently located, and the price is the same whether it is good or poor land. The land we bought was offered for sale only a few weeks before we bought it; we had a presentiment it would be for sale, and watched closely. It is very convenient for us, and much cheaper than other land, as 160 acres cost $200 and a year's time to pay it in. And when the date for payment comes, one must be sure to have the money. If one is only a day tool ate, another can take it from him.

We do not know if we will keep all this land, as we do not have enough money of our own, and it is difficult to borrow such a large sum. Neither do we need so much land for ourselves, and there is no profit in having more land than necessary in these times, when the taxes are so overwhelming on account of the war which is now raging. But if we knew that any of our relatives or friends in Norway would come here, we would try to keep it as long as possible.

We saw in your letter that you wondered how customs were here in America, for example as in weddings. We must answer that customs are as you make them. On our wedding day we did exactly as you do on Tönset at weddings. We went six English miles to church. There are different methods of transportation, sometimes we walk, sometimes we drive oxen and sometimes horses. On our wedding day we drove horses. There are many horses here also, and as in Norway, they may be hired by such as do not own any themselves.

We have both English and Norse school here. We built a large, nice school-house about an English mile from our home, so we have Norse school for a time each year and English school for a time. We have also started Sunday school for the children each Sunday.

A. J. Stortroen

# FOR FURTHER READING

Anderson, Rasmus B. *The First Chapter of Norwegian Immigration (1821–1840), Its Causes and Results.* Published by the author, Madison, 1895.

Blegen, Theodore C. *Land of Their Choice: The Immigrants Write Home.* University of Minnesota: Minneapolis, 1955.

Blegen, Theodore C. *Norwegian Migration to America.* Norwegian-American Historical Association: Northfield, Minnesota, 1931. Reprinted by Arno Press: New York, 1969.

Haugen, Einar I. *The Norwegians in America: A Student's Guide to Localized History.* New York Teacher's College Press: New York, 1967.

Naess, Harold S., and Sigmund Skard, eds. *Studies in Scandinavian–American Interrelations.* American Institute, University of Oslo: Oslo, Norway, 1971.

Nelson, E. Clifford, and Eugene L. Fevold. *The Lutheran Church Among Norwegian-Americans: A History of the Evangelical Lutheran Church.* Augsberg Publishing House: Minneapolis, 1960.

Qualey, Carlton C. *Norwegian Settlement in the United States.* Norwegian-American Historical Association: Northfield, Minnesota, 1938. Reprinted by Arno Press: New York, 1970. Originally a Ph.D. dissertation, Columbia University.

Semmingsen, Ingrid. *Drøm Og Dåd: Utvandringen til Amerika.* H. Aschehaug & Co.: Oslo, Norway, 1975.

Thompson, William F., general editor. *The History of Wisconsin.* 6 volumes. State Historical Society of Wisconsin: Madison, 1973–.

Several Norwegian organizations have placed valuable information about immigration to Wisconsin and the United States on their Web sites. The sites usually include both English and Norwegian versions of the text. "The Promise of America: Norwegian Emigration to America and Norwegian-American History" at http://camilla.nb.no:5000/emigrasjon/emigration contains the texts of books, articles, letters, photographs, film clips, and radio and television broadcasts that relate to Norwegian immigration to America, including many Wisconsin-related titles.

Digitalarkivet (The Digital Archive), a joint project between the National Archives of Norway, the regional Archive of Bergen, and the University of Bergen can be found at http://digitalarkivet.uib.no. Of particular value to Wisconsin researchers is the section of the site labeled "The Norwegian Emigration," http://digitalarkivet.uib.no/ utstilling/eng/main.htm, which contains a database of more than 700,000 Norwegian immigrants to America and includes lists of Norwegian immigrants to Wisconsin compiled from several U.S. censuses. The Web site of the National Library of Norway at http://www.nb.no is also useful. Users should consult the "Norway in America" section of the site, http://www.nb.no/baser/tma/english.html, which contains a searchable bibliography.

# INDEX